MW00886522

DATE: ....

THIS JOURNAL BELONGS TO

....

....

....

....

Made in the USA
Monee, IL
07 January 2022

88310720R00072